KINGFISHER
READERS

Astronauts

Hannah Wilson

KINGFISHER
NEW YORK

KINGFISHER
LONDON & NEW YORK

Copyright © Macmillan Publishers International Ltd 2015
Published in the United States by Kingfisher,
175 Fifth Ave., New York, NY 10010
Kingfisher is an imprint of Macmillan Children's Books, London.
All rights reserved.

Distributed in the U.S. and Canada by Macmillan,
175 Fifth Ave., New York, NY 10010

Library of Congress Cataloging-in-Publication
data has been applied for.

Series editor: Thea Feldman
Literacy consultant: Ellie Costa, Bank Street School for Children, New York

ISBN: 978-07534-7202-6 (HB)
ISBN: 978-07534-7203-3 (PB)

Kingfisher books are available for special promotions
and premiums. For details contact: Special Markets
Department, Macmillan, 175 Fifth Ave., New York, NY 10010.

For more information, please visit
www.kingfisherbooks.com

Printed in China
9 8 7 6 5 4
4TR/0718/WKT/UG/105MA

Picture credits
The Publisher would like to thank the following for permission to reproduce their material.
Every care has been taken to trace copyright holders.
Top = t; Bottom = b; Center = c; Left = l; Right = r
Cover NASA; Pages 4, 5, 6 NASA; 7t, 7b RIA Novosti/Science Photo Library; 8, 9l, 9r NASA; 10 Mark
Paternostro/Science Photo Library; 11l NASA/Science Photo Library; 11r NASA; 12 NASA/Science
Photo Library; 13 RIA Novosti/Science Photo Library; 14 Starsem/Francis Demange/Science Photo Library;
15 NASA/Bill Ingalls; 16 European Space Agency, T. Peake/Science Photo Library; 17, 18t, 18b, 19, 20,
21t, 21b NASA; 22–23 NASA/Science Photo Library; 24–25 NASA; 24b, 25b NASA/Bill Ingalls; 26 NASA/
Science Photo Library; 27 Mark Greenberg/Virgin Galactic/Getty Images; 28 Carol & Mike Werner/Science
Photo Library.

Contents

Brave explorers

Astronauts are highly trained, brave men and women. They are dedicated to helping the world discover what is out in **space** beyond Earth.

Did you know?
"Astronaut" comes from the Greek words for "star" and "sailor."

Since the 1960s astronauts have traveled into space. The first manned flight in a **space capsule** lasted less than two hours. Today, astronauts live and work in huge **space stations** for months at a time.

The National Aeronautics and Space Administration (NASA) in the United States and the European Space Agency run two of the world's space programs.

The first space explorers

At first, no one knew if space would be safe for people. Scientists decided to send animals into space, and see how it affected them. In 1947, fruit flies became the first space travelers! They survived the trip, which lasted only a few minutes.

Ham the Astrochimp
Ham was trained to push levers inside the space capsule.

In 1961, a chimpanzee named Ham spent almost 17 minutes in space. Then his space capsule splashed safely into the ocean.

Yuri Gagarin inside
the capsule

That year, Yuri
Gagarin, a Russian
cosmonaut, became
the first person to
travel into space.

Moon walk

In 1969, Neil Armstrong became the first person to walk on the Moon. He and two other astronauts traveled the more than 238,000 miles (383,000 kilometers) from Earth to the Moon in just three days.

Moon landing
The astronauts traveled down to the surface of the Moon in a small landing craft called *Eagle*.

Footprints made on the Moon's surface will be there forever. There is no wind to cover them up! There is also very little **gravity** on the Moon, so the astronauts felt weightless and bounced above the Moon's surface.

footprint

Famous words
Armstrong's first words on the Moon:
"That's one small step for man, one giant leap for mankind."

Emergency in space!

In 1970, three astronauts were aboard a spacecraft called *Apollo 13*. They were headed to the Moon. Suddenly, there was a loud bang. An **oxygen** tank had exploded! The spacecraft was damaged.

Did you know?
Here's what the astronauts told the control center in Texas after the explosion: "Houston, we've had a problem."

Explosion on board!

The astronauts could not keep going to the Moon. They had to return to Earth. They turned off some equipment to make sure they had enough power to get home. After four days, the space capsule splashed safely down in the Pacific Ocean.

A crane lifts the capsule out of the ocean.

The astronauts arrive home.

Astronaut training

Many people apply to be astronauts. However, only a handful are picked to train. Astronauts need to be good at science, engineering, or math. They need to be physically fit, too.

Vomit comets

An astronaut's training includes time inside an aircraft with reduced gravity. It's called a "vomit comet," because people often get nauseous!

Training takes about two years. Those in training learn how everything on a spacecraft works. They learn how it feels to be in space, too, by doing things like scuba diving in a spacesuit!

On the ground

Thousands of people work hard to get astronauts launched into

Keeping clean
Engineers wear special clothes and hairnets to prevent any dirt or germs from getting into a spacecraft.

space and returned home safely. Engineers design, build, and test spacecraft. Doctors figure out what food, medicine, and exercise the astronauts will need.

During a space trip or mission, a control center, like the one in Houston, closely monitors the spacecraft and maintains contact with the astronauts. The control center is called mission control. Computers track the spacecraft and check its equipment.

Three, two, one, liftoff!

On launch day, the astronauts begin with breakfast. Then they put on their launch suits and take an elevator up to the **cockpit** of the spacecraft.

Launch suits

Astronauts wear special suits during launch and landing. The suits protect them if there is a problem with the oxygen or **air pressure** inside the spacecraft.

The countdown begins,
". . . three, two, one,
liftoff!" The rocket rises
slowly and smoothly
from the launch pad.

The astronauts are pressed
into their seats as the rocket
speeds up. The four boosters
drop away. Then the central
rocket does too. After
nine minutes, the engines
switch off and the
spacecraft floats
in space!

cockpit

central
rocket

booster
rocket

Life on a space station

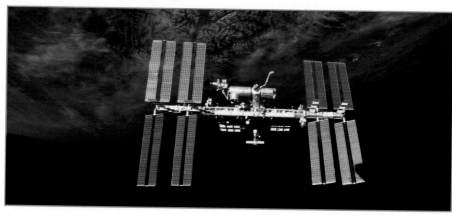

The International Space Station (ISS) is a large spacecraft that **orbits** Earth. It is a science laboratory where astronauts go to do research about life in space.

Bedtime
Astronauts zip themselves into sleeping bags fastened to walls.

Astronauts travel to the ISS in a smaller spacecraft that **docks** with the ISS. There are usually six astronauts living on board. Everything floats unless it is held down— even the food!

All in a day's work

Astronauts might study how plants grow in space. Or, they might make new medicines.

Sometimes the astronauts perform experiments on themselves! They test their eyesight or they take some blood. It's all to help doctors better understand how space travel affects the human body.

When astronauts aren't working, they relax. They read books, watch movies, or play the guitar.

space station

ISS quick facts

Length: 356 feet (111 meters)

Weight: almost 1 million pounds (453,600 kilograms)

spacecraft

Space walk

If something needs repairing on the outside of the space station, it is time for a **space walk**! An astronaut puts on a special spacesuit. The suit includes oxygen, heating and cooling systems, and even a computer.

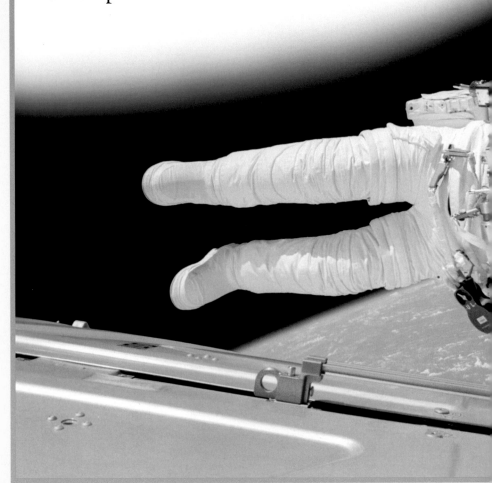

Astronauts leave the space station through two doors. They must lock the first door tightly behind them before opening the second door, so no air escapes from the station.

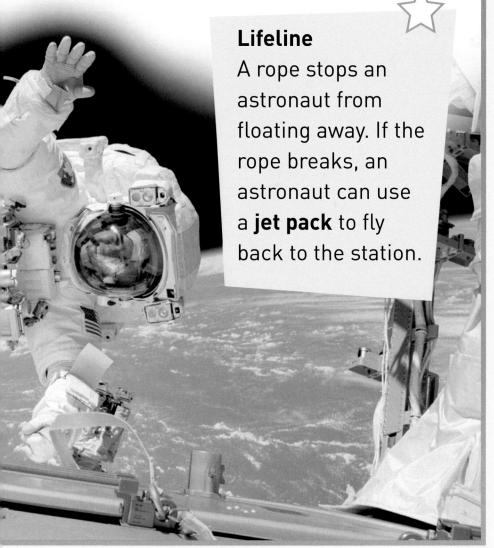

Lifeline
A rope stops an astronaut from floating away. If the rope breaks, an astronaut can use a **jet pack** to fly back to the station.

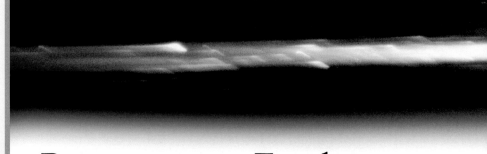

Returning to Earth

A space capsule returning to Earth from the ISS enters the Earth's **atmosphere** so fast it heats the air around it to temperatures around 3,000 °F (1,650 °C)! The capsule has a special heat shield that prevents it from burning up.

Three astronauts are still inside this capsule, which has just landed.

a space capsule entering the atmosphere

Once it is safely inside the atmosphere, parachutes slow down the capsule before it lands. Many space missions have ended with the spacecraft landing in the ocean.

Back on Earth
After returning from space, astronauts rest and have medical check ups.

Space tourists!

Since the first astronauts arrived at the ISS in the year 2000 nearly 200 astronauts from at least eight different countries have stayed on board. Now the ISS sometimes welcomes tourists on board—but the trip doesn't come cheap!

First space tourist
In 2001, Dennis Tito paid about $20 million to spend about six days on the ISS.

Engineers are racing to design new spacecraft for tourists. Tourist spacecraft will not orbit Earth like the ISS. They will travel only just beyond Earth's atmosphere. Here, passengers will experience a few minutes of weightlessness and be able to see the curve of Earth's surface.

This spacecraft can carry six passengers.

The future of space travel

NASA hopes to send astronauts back to the Moon someday. Future plans include the possibility of building a place on the Moon where astronauts could live for up to six months at a time!

Almost every country that has a space program is exploring the idea of sending astronauts to Mars one day. A round trip, there and back, could take up to 18 months!

ASTRONAUT TIMELINE

1961 Yuri Gagarin is the first man in space

1969 Neil Armstrong is the first person
to walk on the Moon

2000 William Shepherd commands the
ISS's first crew

ASTRONAUT RECORDS

Most time spent in space: 803 days
(Sergei Krikalev)

Longest single spaceflight: 438 days
(Valeri Polyakov)

Longest space walk: 8 hours, 56 mins
(Susan Helms and James Voss, 2001)

Youngest astronaut in space: 25 years old
(Gherman Titov, 1961)

Oldest astronaut in space: 77 years old
(John Glenn, 1998)

Glossary

air pressure the force of air pressing down on a person or object

atmosphere gases that surround Earth and make up the air

cockpit the part of a spacecraft where astronauts sit

cosmonaut a Russian astronaut

docks lines up with and parks at a spacecraft

gravity the force that pulls objects toward each other

jet pack a small backpack with a little engine in it that can move an astronaut through space

orbit to continually travel around an object in space

oxygen a gas all living things need to live

space the place that begins about 62 miles (100 km) above Earth

space capsule a small section of a spacecraft, where the cockpit is

space stations large spacecraft and science laboratories that orbit Earth. The International Space Station is the tenth space station

space walk a trip outside a space station or spacecraft to carry out a repair or an experiment

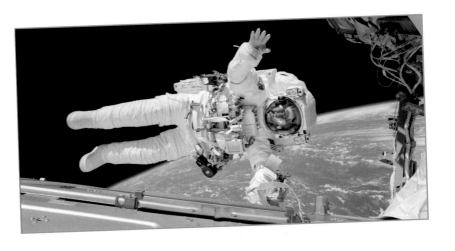

Index